THE STONE GATHERER

for Susan with best wishes
Kristin Philly

For
The Master Craftsman
&
my granddaughter, Zoe Elizabeth.

I would also like to thank the following individuals: George Lamming, my dearest friend and mentor, Edward Baugh, Kamau Brathwaite, Lorna Goodison, Mark McWatt, Elaine Savory, Ramabai Espinet, Elizabeth Nunez, Maria Vasconcelos, Juliet Emanuel, Dana Gilkes, Margaret Gill, Hazel Simmons-McDonald, Jane Bryce, Rob Leyshon, Sherroll Inniss, Rosalind Alleyne, Vivienne Roberts.
Special thanks to Editor Kwame Dawes.

When your children in time to come shall ask the meaning of these stones, then you shall let them know that the Lord your God dried up the waters from before you until you had passed over (Joshua Ch 5: 21-23 KJV paraphrase)

THE STONE GATHERER

ESTHER PHILLIPS

Poetry series editor: Kwame Dawes

P E E P A L   T R E E

First published in Great Britain in 2009
Peepal Tree Press Ltd
17 King's Avenue
Leeds LS6 1QS
UK

ISBN 13: 9781845230852

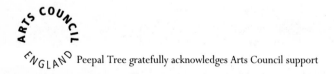 Peepal Tree gratefully acknowledges Arts Council support

CONTENTS

SEER

Pull the caul backwards
over her face lest she see spirits.
May the ancestors never vex
her with their half-aborted dreams.
Let her see only the clear blue
of sky or water, never the boiling
red, the murky green-black Atlantic.

Set her gaze forward,
never backward; never fixed within
a space grown dumb by suffering.
Her dreams at midnight should be
sweet, ephemeral as cloud.
But cursed with second-sight
she may perceive her face within
the lineaments of those who haunt
her; she may stretch forth her hand
to free their chattering tongues.

Pull the caul backwards over her face.
Let it come gentle, clean over her eyes,
leave no trace.

The seer cannot help but hear.
But let it not be the fresh cry
of forests, the sound of the zebra,
the great lion's roar.
Close her ears to the echoing call
under the drum's rhythm ancient
as blood. Cut her memory clean
as her navel-string; let the ocean-
salt cure history and memory.

II

Hers must be the lexicon
of the New World. It best suits here —
where the ground of faith shifts
with each new dawn, and none
discerns the root from branch
or blighted leaf. Better she be half-
blind, better she not hear portents
rising from sea-rocks or the battling
waves. Let her not hear under the
fulsome cry of the marketplace,
the gathering spirits whisper —
    Lest she should speak.

According to folklore, a child born with a caul (web-like membrane covering
the face) would be gifted with second-sight. This gift could remain or be lost
depending on how the caul was removed at birth.

MASK

…until my sister, ever tactless, said,
'*You're assuming that you're a great man.*'
And the words fled from the room,
dodged the mad wheels of summer
motorcyclists, slapped the flags
hoisted for the Labor Day Parade,
ripped bunting from storefronts,
skimmed like a skate up the Hudson,
slid past the currents threatening
to swallow them up; howled like a skin-
salted higue over the Brooklyn Bridge,
rose higher, higher, wailing, drumming
on windows no one would open.

And I, who'd helped him dream
this greatness, could not speak.
While his thick fingers stretched
the accordion out like long lost years.
And he, pretending not to hear
my sister's words, spoke on.

Brooding in every corner
of the room, the lumbering shadow
formed itself into a question:
Why? Why this? What way
to reconcile my father, proud, erect,
dressed in his well-pressed suits,
keeping his Cadillac in mint condition?
What way to understand the squalor
he returned to every day?
'*No words,*' she'd said, '*there are no words
that can describe the horror.
No wonder he has kept us out.*'

He'd finished his stories
of illustrious men, their deprivations,
great deeds they'd left behind them.
He played his final favourite hymn,
finding the notes by instinct, as it seemed:
'*Now the day is over, night is drawing nigh
Shadows of the evening steal across the sky.*'
How often had he looked into the shapes
behind the shadows? How often had he seen
among whatever demons haunted him,
his children, whom he said he'd loved
and left so many years ago?

II

Perhaps for him another kind of greatness:
to straddle two opposing worlds
and find some foothold; to gaze
into the heart of his own darkness,
square his shoulders and walk on;
never to say, "This punishment
is more than I can bear."

Sitting this summer evening in this
Brooklyn room my sister laboured
to restore, what does it matter now?
We look behind the mask.
And choose to love him still.

LEGACY

My mother's touch was not tender.
Everything was *fortissimo*. She made no
gentle overtures, slipping with graceful ease
on to a polished stool; a cane-bottomed chair
held her full weight. Hers were not long,
tapering fingers, slightly curved to show

the artistic mind; her fingers were short and thick,
broken nails sheltering bits of earth.
I knew by the set of her jaw and the sad aura
around her, it was not just the piano
my mother played: a score was more like some-
thing she needed to settle – a mere slip
and a chord could betray her.

And the way she sang in her kind of *larghetto:*
"O my darling, O my darling Clementine,
Thou art lost and gone forever, dreadful sorry, Clementine,"
her farewell to a girlhood gone too soon.
Now husbanding her crop of children,
she wrested from a trap of horizontal spaces
what melody she could.

Years later in an unyielding season
and far away from home,
I listen for the slightly out-of-tune piano
and see her as I did not then:
Seed-Mother, beginner of life, of Art,
out of the cumber she bore painter, dancer, poet.
Her sad songs lured us into feeling
for word, image, rhythm to shape our world.

VIOLET

for the old woman in the window

In the crab-crawl of morning
when SUV must humble
like any old smoke-
farting van in the long,
long line to Bridgetown,
and a quarrel from last night
have every chance to flare
up again, and the children
complaining which teacher
they hate and they sorry
the weekend finish –

*"Mornin', how wunnuh? How
de family? De road busy enough
dis mornin'. Tek yuh time, hear?
Tek it easy. De lord bless yuh."*

And all of a sudden,
how so much memory
could rush from one chattel-house
window, could fill up a SUV quick
so with oil-leaf smell and Vicks
and candle-grease, and a small
boy scarcely able to breathe,
and an old woman rubbing
his back and chest and rocking
him back and forth, back and
forth, *"Dohn mind, tek it easy,
you tek it easy."*

He didn't know when
he'd got used to seeing her,
this woman he had never met,

until one morning, underneath
her window, a sign: VIOLET IS DEAD.
Perhaps some neighbour thought
that passersby should know her name.
So late, for some had named her already:
to the poet, she was the muse of a past
long gone, to the blind, perhaps
just some crazy old woman.

But oil-leaf smell and Vicks and all,
she's with him in the boardroom now.
When he would jump ahead the line, nudge
a partner back down a rung or two,
he hears his Gran-Gran's voice: "*Tek it easy.*
Tek yuh time, hear. De Lord bless yuh."

A KIND COVERING

This morning under the beat
of rain and ever-slowing
traffic, it hums its slow
prelude, rises
resolute against
any other movement,
except for this:

small children drenched
and going home from school.
We walk along a narrow
marl-road, its sides flaky
from rain, hedgerows
smeared chalky,
sage bush pungent and black.

This gloomy evening
hides a keen bright edge;
a double-terror: Ol' John,
the red-eyed heart-man,
mad grave-digger.
He may be sheltering
in a cave, just off the track
next to the 'fustic' vines.
Our shouts rival the distant
thunder as we race by.

No wind stirs the canes
beside the main road.
They lean, weary
from the rain's lashing,
and for us the journey is long.

"Look Granny!
Look Granny parasol coming!"

As we huddle around her,
wearing old jackets she brought,
something of soft light
and soundless air circles
above us, invisible, inviolate;
in the midst her quiet murmur ...
"...*the secret place... Most High...*
Shadow of the Almighty."

Over time and distance,
in tumult worse than any weather,
there comes on a windchant
her blessing spoken over us:
He shall cover thee... He shall cover thee...
and under His wings shalt thou trust.

MILO

The other day my grown and married daughter
said to me, "I sound like this because I have the flu.
Daddy's on his way over here. But he might be

at the supermarket now. I guess he's buying Milo."
"Milo?" I asked? "Yes," she said chuckling,
"he buys me Milo whenever I'm sick.

In fact, it doesn't matter what I'm sick with.
A while ago the weather changed.
I got bronchitis and he bought me Milo.

He bought me Milo when they lost my papers
and I had to have that vaccine all over again.
And the day they came and towed away Plym

and I cried (her first car had finally died)
or when I've just had a bad day.
In fact, I've got tins of it in my cupboard."

And I think to myself,
I might have saved a good deal
of my marriage to this guy, had I known.
Back then I'd given him love,
much talk and copious tears, when Milo,
cups and cups of it might have done the job!

Sweetheart, should you run out of room
in your cupboard,
keep the space in your heart open;
that's what he's after.

.

TRANSITION RADIO

(on breaking the news to a renowned writer
that someone had stolen his German-
made Grundig radio while in my keeping)

Don't get vex, love,
is you who praise Caliban
fuh tiefin words from European.
Talk 'bout battle fuh language,
talk 'bout struggle,
you should see how small de space is
he come through! He tek out louvres,
scale a wall (active process
and historic mission!).
So yes, he tief de Grundig radio
dat you used to own,
but think 'bout all de language
now in Caliban possession:
    de BBC world news,
    de latest book reviews
    all dat learned discourse
    on global upheaval
    political and social —

Pardon me?

By now the thief must have sold
the damned radio for just a few dollars?

Well… when it comes to language,
ain't you the one who see continuing
possibility? Caliban just expanding
his options. It is cultural emancipation,
love, is culture in transition.

MY BROTHER

A little boy ran down
the road with a roller,
his magic metal wand
striking mirrored
memories of you,
my brother.

How often did your
bare feet hammer
your frustration into
this hot tar, insistent
hands striking, every
lash echoing your own pain,
willing with furrowed brow
and glinting tears the roller
to go straight, for so might
your own stifled dreams
one day run straight and true?

What gadgets do you play
with now, brother? Time
Machines? Computers?
Do you drive your high-
powered car with surer aim
down paved highways,
your eyes glinting blood
and steel so that I hardly know you?

For a moment now you're pushing
your roller back down the road.
But as it swerves off-course,
I rescue it for you
I right it for you
I hand it back to you
and you smile at me.

UNWRITTEN POEM

You never gave me time
to write your poem.
I needed time to know you:
the fledgling husband playing
his unaccustomed role,
no model given from the past;

your hip-hop scene, what lines
or rhythms hooked your soul
until you felt all that was earth
and heaven pulsed within this music;
what zeal, what rebel songs
ignited you, your manhood,
your secret passions into being.

When should I have written your poem?
The day of your wedding?
when you, handsome in tuxedo,
took her hand and swore
that you would love her always?

Would it have been the day
you placed my grandchild in my arms?
For in that very moment, my heart
would have soared upwards.

Or when we strolled the summer
morning in the woods, and laughed
at makeshift walking sticks,
cleared a few vines, picked
some wild flowers for my daughter,
talked of dirt-bikes, old relics,
nothing in particular;
just glad a woman and her son-in-law
could have no discord.

Should it have been the night
I stood behind your sleeping form
and prayed with all the fervour of my heart,
my right hand stretched towards you?
And deep in your unconscious sleep,
you stretched your right hand out

and held it still, suspended, under mine.
I did not speak for fear of waking you,
nor could you see me in the darkness
where I stood. I never will forget
the strange, transcendent moment.

But now you're gone,
and all the hopes I cherished, prized,
will flourish in the gaze of someone else's eyes.
How does the heart recover from the lives
we've met and touched? So little time,
so little time, yet loved so much.

CEREMONY OF INNOCENCE

*(on a photograph   in the newspapers
taken on Kadooment Day)*

Receive them, receive
the little children.
Let the butt-stringed
mama clutch the boy
and push his face
between her breasts
that suckled infant boys.
Bump and grind him,
Mama, jam the fledg-
ling, juck the nine-year
yout'-man. Teach him
your rhythms of
    woman-rage
    woman-hunger
    woman-need,
your own kadooment
in disguise. Now set him
down and watch your seed
spill from his eyes.

II

Receive the little children;
draw her with
gentle-seeming cords.
Break her frail sparrow-
bones. Bring her spread-
eagled, mingle her blood
with semen of fathers
and uncles; take from
her eyes forever
the light of laughter –

Better she had drowned
in innocent womb-water.

Where is the children's
heritage? Where on this
earth their kingdom of heaven?

Let the stone hewn by the mill
be summoned, and the necks
of offenders carry the burden.
May the seabed rise to meet them.

* kadooment — a kind of carnival.

BIRD CATCHER

I caught a dove darkening the dawn
with her brooding,
grieving the loss of the cold ark.
I let her fly near the light
of the bright green lime tree,
the gleaming red hibiscus.
Now some days she leaves off
her mourning, and the song
she sings from the healing
olive tree is her trilogy of peace.

Small brown bird, making your way
over Lake Osceola,
for your dull feathers I gave you
bright metallic blue, and the sun,
taking no notice of you before,
startled itself into laughter:
how sudden your flight, your
sapphire streak on grey water!

I caught an egret flying westward
and it became a faithless heart,
(forgive me, winged creature!)
I watched it falter, beating empty air.
I knew the egret's wings would fold
to rest the weary bird. Rising again,
he'd find his sure way homeward.

A cry broke free from a spectrum
of colour at sunset and I shaped it
to a memory of love.
It was the high-soaring sea gull.
I gave my love to the flight
of the bird, the call of the air.
It would return a purer love some day.

The birds within my poems, friend,
they fly unhindered by my pen,
not plundered for easy merchandise,
shot from the sky,
caught only in my cage of fantasy.

RUNNER

(for young poet, Ben Zimman Bright)

Do not fear for your heart;
you were born for running,
you who pluck consonants
like silver from the generous
air, move in metred syllables
along the nerves to quicken
memory, waken vision.

Yours is the ready sympathy,
the quick flight to the ancient
wound; the hill-bound angel
who knows no comfort.
Behind the girl in henna-
patterned hands you stand,
your eyes a mirror,
knowing her betrothed
may never love her.

Still restless as you watch
the wreck of others' lives,
you journey to the world of in-
between: the adolescent ache
for knowledge, the lonely drunk
returning home, the hyped-up girls
trailing black marigolds or lost
among the brine-washed roses.

Wide traveller, you've felt so soon
the chilling touch of your own frailty,
but you're the runner for whom the thought
of death should have no fear – not you,
whose prescient heart outleaps the light year.

LACUNA
(for John Balaban)

Let there always be the space
that nothing fills completely.
If the only home I have
is one my art invents,
then let there ever be
some bed or chair empty.
Let the gold or purple
streak or the green flash
perfecting sunset not
appear, or may they come
seconds before my eyes
had turned to see.

I do better in the gap
the interruption
the pause
between
a word spoken

and its meaning;
a love missed,
a rhythm
common as breath

broken.

It is the interlude
It is the interlude
that I can fix
or fashion as I choose.

PRISM

Between the gentle irony
and the vastness of truth
are the eyes
that always look surprised
when others touch
the mirror's hardness
and feel secure;
for souls are meant to go
beyond senses.

Veils over eyes
should rather be bound
tightly over
fingertips.

THE SCEPTIC
(for Michael)

He who trusts nothing,
thinks religion, the saving
of the soul, arrant nonsense,
he takes a loft not good
for anything, and by a "self-
inflicted cleaning", as he puts it,
purges the muck, old rubbish,
clinging cobwebs. "Incredible,"
he said, "you'd never guess
the junk we store over years."

The stairs his Dolorosa,
he heaves and strains
under the weight of
horizontal timbers,
upright beams.
On hands and knees
he cuts and shapes
for walls not square,
rafters gone askew.
Then up the ladder
he hauls dry wall
with groans, great drops
of sweat.

He's put the joists in
seven inches deep,
the perfect buttress
fit to bear the weight
of those who'll tarry there;
five horizontal beams,
the sign of grace, above
the heads of those who

climb the stairs;
three windows sealed
against the rain and wind,
but threefold source
to let the Sun come in.
Then he covers all
in pristine white
and blots out every flaw.

One day, they'll catch him, unawares,
pushing the skylight... gazing heavenward.

POT-MAKER

So she gathers her fragments,
the ruins of her story.
Last night she walked, diviner
among the pieces, made covenant
with them that they would live;
she swore by the cuts on her hands
and the stain of her blood.

Like a casuarina in the east wind,
her back flattens so all the ages
may come to rest upon her.
And in the shadows of her face,
her hand, the men she moulded
in her womb, still wait to drink from her.

Where is the shelter they have built
for her treasures, the beauty of her craft,
the strength of her labours?
Only a hut stripped, posts fragile against
the storm? A soon-coming dark?

She asks no such questions. She knows
creativity is collision: she knows a vessel
can never come whole from the earth.

HIGUE

A new moon hangs like a limpid flame
in the cold and quiet darkness of the night.
Below the cliff, the feel of salt
on the wind prickling the skin.
From the tamarind tree a late dove calls:
Something on edge in the air.

What is this presence in the air?
Her lantern bears a yellow flame.
If you should hear her calling
when you walk alone at night,
remember how she got her filmy skin
and why she dreads the smell of salt.

But now she braves her fear of salt.
Weaving her magic on the captive air
she lures a young man with her glowing skin.
Bewitched, he turns to follow her flame,
falls over the cliff to his death in the night:
another soul lost to her dreadful calling.

The mother does not hear the late dove's call;
no rice grains on her steps, no bag of salt.
Higue sucks the baby's blood in the dark of night,
his single cry lost on the cooling air.
Her eyes shine bright as yellow flame;
the little body left with palest skin.

Hurry higue! It's nearly sunrise! Find your skin!
Delay and you may lose your dreaded calling.
Oh agony! Fiercer than any flame:
they've found her skin, packed it with salt
like a huge wound. Her sharp cries pierce the air
and shatter what's left of the night.

The sun comes up, stripping the cover of night.
Under a tree, a drying wrinkled skin.
Higue casts yet one more spell into the air,
desperate to resist this final call.
But higue succumbs to the awesome power of salt.
She disappears in a raging ball of flame.

Higue poet! calling words like flame
through the night air, probing deep under the skin,
baring her wounds to the salt of words.

UNSEEN

Often there
in your river-surge
of voice
like silt, like debris
diverging
through twisted roots;
I heard them
when in your deep-
throated discourse
you debated them,
sometimes with loud
passion
or in a mere whisper.
I saw them
in your careful scrutiny
of my face, the sudden
shifting of your eyes,
a quick smile hidden,
not to be shared.

They were sent to bind
your heart, your tongue.
Cleft-handed,
they loosed your brain
only for seasons.

But I know them now.
I do not fear them.
I am my grand-
mother's child
and she was
a demon-fighting woman.
I heard her cry out
on her knees.

I saw her tarry
on mission hall floors,
lips cracked from fasting,
until one day
a wing-rush:
Heaven open
hex gone
and look how
river flow free
with a clear shining.

THE GARDENER

*...in this moment, there is life and food
for future years ('Lines Written Above Tintern Abbey' —
W. Wordsworth*)

The last of summer flowers
will always be the last of summer
flowers. The iris, rose, sweet
columbines will wither and fall.
Chrysanthemums must soon
yield up their autumn-gold,
and pansies, braving the winter's
frost, may yet succumb to the worm
or otherwise expire. And since
we plant new seeds for every season,
it's never exactly the same garden.

But always the same seeking — always —
to hold still the moment of beauty
— the fragrance, colour, interplay of light —
when all we are or feel ourselves to be
is silent, comes to attention, bending
towards the inner ear, striving to hear
the quiet rhythm running along
the nerves, released into the noiseless
air around us, ever elusive...

But as the river to its source, the wing
of the butterfly to its Designer,
so the silence of the moment
to its Maker who willed it so: beauty
with desire, that we, hungry for meaning
sensed behind reality, may track Him through
the silence, the moment none interprets — only He.

VENDOR

Bunches of coconuts
at the side of the road
and a gate locked behind
them. Then after two days
of no takers, a sign marked, "Free."

You know what free is, Mister?
The right to be decent:
to knock on the door of a neighbour
or two and ask if they would like
some coconuts, and (if they do)
open your gate so they could
go inside and get them.

What do you fear? You think
next morning you may have
to say, "Good morning?"
Or your neighbours might expect
an invitation to your house?

Listen, those coconuts you left
at the side of the road aren't free;
they're tainted from the root
by your disease, the prejudice
that masks itself as generosity.
Your faceless gesture marks
a man locked in the old contagion
of his race – not free, not free at all.

JACOB PRIEST

Face wrung with the grief
of an overburdened heart,
he hears again his half-truths
couched in jargon, his artful
exhortations in tribute
to the god of mammon.

But it is Sunday.
He, the shepherd, now must lead,
must stand behind the pulpit
calling the people to repentance.

Not for him another private
penance, a secret wrestling,
flesh over spirit, the silent anguish
whispered many times before.
Today, he'll humble himself
before the people, kneel with
the worst of them down at the altar.

A young man, blind, seeing
only priest and shepherd, inter-
cepts him, and placing his hand
upon the young man's head
the shepherd prays for him; and then another
stands in line, and then another –
the shepherd's moment for repentance gone.

What would he give for one discerning soul
among the flock; for one wise heart to strip,
tear, wrench him from the prison
into which they've locked him!

CONTRARIES

A flock of egrets trailed
a silent grace across a pearl-grey sky,
burst the clouds and broke
the quiet morning chant
into discord.

The wind complained,
not in the mango or banana
trees, but on housetops
in the restless wings of doves:

a mix-up morning.

It was a day like this
some village men decide
to move the house of God
from rent to buy-land;
even the angels should rejoice.
But no, the roof fall down
and kill Tom Johnson.

The story is, the man
was wicked, couldn't stand
church people, and years ago
(he must be forget!),
he wish by the oath
the church would fall
pon de bunch o' hypocrites.

Not a soul call him that morning.
He step right up to lend a hand,
grab a corner, lost his balance
and meet his end.
Just so!

CONTRARIES II

Somewhere
a namer and shaper
watches a sunrise
walks by the sea
savours colour
form and motion.

But underneath
she feels the snarl
the mix-up
the uncertain justice
the darkness
none can apprehend
that ever lurks
to drive the poet's pen.

ACT III

Girls who are like their fathers
and subject to Jehovah's wrath
are not supposed to smile.
So she cracks up inside when they
take her serious face seriously;
or swear by her purity
since she always sits up straight;
her ethical brace barely touching
the back of the chair.

She paints herself at times in garish
reds and blues only the farsighted
can see; juggles 'Thou shalt nots'
behind her back and lets them drop.
She loses her balance on a tightrope
and none can tell the difference.

Her favourite act? The tigress tamed
and jumping through the hoops.
The fire tempers her edge,
reconfigures her nerves at the crack
of the whip. She's knows the exact
moment when their gaze, their courage
slips. She's waiting. Ready.

GUILT

Between the silent Seraphim,
Wings overarching me,
I kneel before Your Mercy Seat.

Oh, do not speak, I fear
Your anger; I cannot bear
The censure in Your voice.

Commune with me,
Your great Heart to
My trembling heart.

Feel my love torn,
The greater portion Yours
And still shall always be.

The rest is his, and he
And I are flesh — eyes, lips,
Hands and thighs, and sweetness.

Do not forsake me,
Oh, do not cast me off!
Was it for love *You* died
That I might live —
And love?

NIGHT ERRANT

You hate the ignoble
thing, the unworthy.
You believe man is
the measure (despite
your brilliance.)
So when the wolf rips
the night open,
the night you had so drawn
with soft colours,
you deny, you deny,
you deny.
And the creature,
on cue, disappears;
the air, snarled, lies
heavy between us.

I've not much use
for a cerebral-shaped heart
nurtured on some one-eyed
philosophy.

Love me with your own
heart hoarding the traitor,
the rough rage, your un-
certain compassion.

NEXUS

You wear your need for me
like an affliction; some strange dis-
ease that overtook you unawares.
This need is your undoing,
this can't-wait-to-hear-her-voice-once-more
madness, your frenzy that would force
the hours to leap the two long days
since seeing her and seeing her again.

I am your loss of style:
the sad cessation of your old war-cry,
"Pursuer never, always pursued."
I am your dotage, your vulnerable
season. This need defies your old
philosophies, disputes your proven
forms of reasoning. You swear sometimes
I am your Nemesis, even.

I fear the day, my love,
when you should think this need
a burden that you cannot bear.

Be patient. Here is no sorcery,
no duplicitous entanglement.
The Hand that guided me to you
and you to me is stronger than my own.
A higher wisdom pre-contrives
the meeting of improbabilities.
So anxious need transformed
by love may rest at ease.

PASSION

By now these white walls
should be bright fluorescent
pink, deep purple, climbing
all over themselves; these tiles
should curl at the edges
when I walk. I'm surprised
I don't short-circuit the TV;
scorch the wings off Dali's
butterflies above my bed.
Cixous must have been joking;
I'd gladly take the sceptre. Now.
My patience long-exhausted
prefers another monument
and will no longer smile at grief.
Self-help's a contravention
Onan tried, we know what happened.
No recourse in the old cold shower,
with all these taps just spewing hot water.
Wuh loss!!... Wuh *lossssss!!!!*

AND YET AGAIN

Tonight I want to offer you
this moonlight cupped in a purple
flower; this chorus of crickets
holding no grudge against the day's
dying. I want to lift the cool sweetness
of sour-grass under the night wind
and soothe the tautness in your face.
I want to tempt you away from your heroic
silence for joy that is free and foolish.
I want to weave these early stars
like a rope for you to hold
and make your way past your old
hurts, faiths crumbling like dust.
This wanting is not a nebulous thing;
it is the soul desiring its other self
where need knows no hindrance of words.

Now, only this longing, this reaching
yet again — in spite of.

LESSON

(For students: Melanie, Stacy-Ann and Shaniqua)

Not all noise and adolescent posturing
or sentences derailed between full-stops,
or the eternal enmity of subject and verb;
three students have come to throw roses
on the grave of an old woman
they never knew; enough for them that she
was Ma'am's grandmother whom she loved.

One in black trousers and long-sleeved shirt,
takes seriously – by her expression – this burden
of sympathy. The other, demure, holds
her skirt close, steps up to the grave, throws
her red rose. The last, so deeply
pensive, tears running.

This strange parody: young students
months away from Graduation stand
in silence, while just across from them,
a group all dressed in purple caps and gowns
burst into song, a slab of stone their platform –
and bridging these two, an open grave...

...a flick of a page and Ophelia's casket closes
Blanche stays forever locked in Old World fantasies
Marx and all theorists banished to shelf or book-bag...

But this September afternoon between sun and shadow,
the sound of stones falling on a wooden coffin,
a teacher is undone by grief for a grandmother
who was to her (as theirs to them, no doubt)
an anchor and a certain solace.

I place an arm around the young girl's shoulders
and ask, half guessing, "Who're you remembering?"
Between her sobs she answers,
"My boyfriend... they killed 'im... in June."

And suddenly the evening slams hard
against the peaceful passing of an old
woman and all other assumptions.

Yes. Face it. This is their world
of anger, knives and guns; the bloody graffiti
on walls and pavements. Old age? A peaceful
death? Grandmother's God ensuring justice
against the wicked? Not for them. Not for them.

COMMON ENTRANCE

Her father walks away, stifling
thoughts of homicide. Her mother
sits dejected. Last week Daneille
knew everything, today
Daneille knows nothing...
or so they think.

And while her peers wait anxiously
for places in top schools,
dream of prizes for best student,
being prefect or head girl,
or athlete of the year,
she makes no such assumptions:

"Auntie, I don't care which school,
as long as they don't wear brown shoes."
All her life she's worn them,
she complains; she simply
cannot wear brown shoes again.

While the world rocks
with the weight of urgent decisions,
reels from the shock of disappointed
hope, frustrated yearning, sad despair,
one girl walks free of presumption
clear-eyed and even-keeled.

WORD

(On teaching an adult male to read)

He trusted me to break
the word, crack each segment
open until the mystery expired.
Not so this morning;
he stared bewildered
at the board then back at me:
"I never t'ought dat word
could be so small... F-i-x,"
he mused, *"dis word so small."*

How could his daily toil
of hammer, saw and nails;
an old lady's reckoning
of last month's window
against the patching
of her roof this week –
how could her life of sacrifice
and his of labour, sweat
and boiling sun
be totalled up
in this small word?

CLOTHES HANGER

In a deep and treacherous corner,
from breadfruit trees, mango trees,
a woman's dresses hanging everywhere;
red, blue, green, can't miss them.
In fact, it's clear we're meant to see them.
Which woman would hang her
clothes at the side of the road like that?

They say it's her son who put them there
– his mother died just recently –
but what is the shape of this grief?
Perhaps she's too much in the house,
still lying on the bed or sitting on a chair.
It's more than he can bear alone,
so passersby must let him share it.

Last week, he put her chamber pot
right on the bush. Open-faced.
For all to see. Well, now, I wonder…
Bright dresses, yes, but long-sleeved,
high-necked, full-length to the ground.
So why does he expose her?
Some anger he has buried for too long?
Some wounds inflicted over years, hidden
and deep, his only chance for vengeance
now she's gone? *"Well, yuh know,
de young man head ain't right."*
Well, yes, and so I wonder.

EASY-BOY

A breath, a shadow,
he is himself the passing of years
so softly he walks; bare feet
intimate with dust, the debris of dreams.

He is a friend of birds;
their flight though swift
is noiseless too.
Perhaps he's learnt
what many kings
and rulers never knew:

Walk easy. Measure your stride
against the changeful winds,
lest you awaken what you may not
put to sleep again.

Cast off your hobnailed boots,
your sandals borrowed from Colossus.
Walk softly where the poor
and humble weep. Such ground is holy.

Sit some days on the fence, if you will,
like the lonely egret, brooding, still,
and hear beneath the noise of men
the hush of your own passing.

ARRIVAL

Why now, why now this
evening time when, as you say,
our flag is flying at half-mast?
And Captain, O my Captain,
what is this cargo that you bring me?
Stones of sapphire turning to stars
between your fingers? Rubies
gleaned where the river bends
at Belle Vue, Sans Souci?

Such was the bounty you brought
another love who counted with leaves,
tender and green from the woods
in spring, your vows of homecoming.
I could have told her,
Oh, I could have told her, leaves
wither and glass houses splinter.

I too have gathered
stones on a faraway shore
where the hurricane's eye,
swollen, slept for a moment,
and I gathered stones to mark my praise.

And shall I tell you?
Will you believe me when I tell you
that on that day I dreamed I saw the pebble
you had hidden under the grape-leaf?
I saw it changed, crystallized
into W/word and into meaning.

If you would know this meaning,
come with me not far along this shore,
where grape trees cut a path

by the sandbank. There you will hear
a voice ancient with knowing
that a man, weary from seeking,
may find at last what he once sought
in the arms of lovers,
in the wide ocean's heart,
in the pride of reason:

a pebble changed into a pearl

And for this Pearl he trades
his other kingdoms.

BIRTHDAY VISIT TO CUBA

How the skies spoke on your birthday!
the same reverberations I've heard
in your voice. Only, this morning
there's an ellipsis in the echo.

For these ten days you're harvest-
ing memories I cannot share.
You are bone-gathering:
a fist once folded in defiance,
the feet that spurned an empire
hobbled now among grave stones;
a headband red as Rodney's blood
bleached by the years' indifference.

They fete you, as they rightly should.
While the young and bright pay tribute
to title and tenure, you sit, half-listening,
honing your reluctant peace.

You see how the *Beast* may win after all:
its subterranean smell invades the city
in the half smirk on the cashier's face;
the branding of appetite with cell phones
and DVD players; the brag of steel
and chrome over iron, cracked but enduring,
a barter of nation for capital illusion.

When you return, I'll have a meal,
a change of clothing, a space for luggage ready for you.
But there's not room enough to house the ashes
your eyes may speak of.

PAPER TRAILING
(for a writer in his 80th year)

I'd thought that for all
your sorting, tearing,
putting aside,
you were content
in your *stable*.
You and paper
have held each other
hostage for decades
on end, a familiar torment —

until, belly sickened
with words,
you'd let the page
have it! green, black,
yellow bile forging,
reshaping islands,
sinking empire;
and in the terror of the moment,
the page yielded, multiplied.

I'm not so sure
what this putting aside,
sorting, tearing might mean now —
Clearing out?

A PRECIPITATE SORROW

I live too much in the now, the flame
the thunder of you. When you are gone,
how often will I turn an evening's silence
into a rosary, coaxing the past with crystal
beads, if only… if only…
How will I unhear, untouch memory?
How dilute your gaze, remove
its essence, like the years' varnish,
from all we loved?

Perhaps the mystery dimmed now
by the familiar will come again,
and distance (the endless exile!)
will draw you closer beyond
the feel of flesh.

After months have passed,
when it's only the wind and my fingers
turning the pages, I'll read your
conversations of age and innocence again.

No longer your bright shadow
over my shoulder, the lucent filter
of your mind to clarify, expand,
yet every message, each edict
amplified by absence.

I'm told I should ask all the questions
now, record word and gesture,
nuance and circumstance,
as if Time were mine to mediate,
devise moment with meaning, arrange
or label for future conveyers of history.

And yet, I negotiate: make a dry-run
of tomorrow's grief against the long, slow
hours when I shall wish my heart a palimpsest.

ABOUT THE AUTHOR

Esther Phillips holds an MFA degree in Creative Writing from the University of Miami where she won the Alfred Boas Poetry Prize of the Academy of American Poets. Her first collection of poems appeared in chapbook form and was published by the University of the West Indies in 1983. She also won the Frank Collymore Literary Endowment Award (first prize) for her collection, *When Ground Doves Fly* (Ian Randle Publishers, 2003). Her work has appeared in several journals and anthologies in the Caribbean, the USA and the U.K. These include *The Whistling Bird: Caribbean Women Writers* and *Blue Latitudes: Caribbean Women Writers at Home and Abroad*. Esther Phillips is Head of the Division of Liberal Arts at the Barbados Community College, is a member of the Frank Collymore Literary Endowment Committee and is editor of *BIM: Arts for the 21st Century*.

PRAISE FOR THE STONEGATHERER

'These poems are strong, meditative, complex and crafted with a meticulous eye for detail.Spiritual and philosophical insights are refracted through the prism of Caribbean folklore and ways of seeing that are unique to the Region. An intense and revelatory collection of poetry for our times!'

Ramabai Espinet

In these poems about ordinary people and relationships (father, mother, daughter, ex-husband, neighbour) Esther Phillips treats human emotions like buildings, rooms, into which she moves with ease, assessing their state of repair and their impact upon her with a shrewd and calculating eye. In this way she achieves a graceful mastery, often leaving the reader in shock, not only at the fact that she has led him/her so effortlessly into these intricate interior spaces of love, fear, regret and forgiveness; but also that she deftly indicates, in spare and supple verse, the surest way out of these labyrinths. the reader's response is a sense of gratitude and understanding – and a deep admiration for the poet.

Mark McWatt

Esther Phillips is one of the best Caribbean poets writing today. Her rhythms and images capture the uniqueness of her Caribbean identity and character.

Elizabeth Nunez

This collection's great theme is the infinite variety and strength of love, tested, disappointed, celebrated, and only able to be captured through the agency of supple, deeply thoughtful language. Esther Phillip's delicate, subtle and wonderfully crafted poems, spare but richly nuanced, construct a multi-dimensional emotional world. In these poems, the belief is that art bears important witness to our complex humanity, not just through expressing the capacity to feel, but also, gently, what it is to know and explain what we feel, not just through the ability to make but also, without flinching, what it is to make and to break, to have and to lose that which we value. They consider by turns women, men and nature, sometimes with humor, sometimes with fear, sometimes with concern tinged with anxiety, very often with affection, in lyric voices which represent the human or the supernatural or both together. Their variety of theme and perspective is matched by their diverse structural identities, so that each poem has its particular and special way of speaking its concerns in both form and content. This is a fine body of work, a delight to read and savour.

Elaine Savory

Marion Bethel
Bougainvillea Ringplay
ISBN: 9781845230845; pp. 88, July 2009; £7.99

These poems are sensual in the most literal sense – the poems are about the senses, the smell of vanilla and sex, the sound of waves – radio, voices, sea; the taste of crab soup; the texture of hurricane wind, and the chaos of colours bombarding the eye. Bahamian poetry is being defined in the work of Marion Bethel.

Jacqueline Bishop
Snapshots from Istanbul
ISBN: 9781845231149; pp. 80, April 2009; £7.99

Framed by poems that explore the lives of the exiled Roman poet Ovid, and the journeying painter Gaugin, Bishop locates her own explorations of where home might be. This is tested in a sequence of sensuous poems about a doomed relationship in Istanbul, touching in its honesty and, though vivid in its portrayal of otherness, highly aware that the poems' true subject is the uprooted self.

Frances Marie Coke
Intersections
ISBN: 9781845230845; pp. 106, August 2009; £7.99

Francis Coke writes with eloquent empathy and profound insight about the difficult truths of family relations, abandonment, loneliness, and the challenges of faith when hope is hard to find. She writes about Jamaica's poverty, violence, class divides and racial complexities with the same tenderness that she writes about its people.

Mahadai Das
A Leaf in His Ear
ISBN: 978900715591; pp. 160, May 2009; £9.99

The selection includes the whole of *Bones* and *My Finer Steel Will Grow*, and most of the poems from her first collection, *I Want to Be a Poetess of My People*, as well as many of the fine poems published in journals and previously uncollected – from lively, humorous nation-language poems to the oblique, highly original poems written in the years after *Bones*.

Kwame Dawes
Hope's Hospice
with images by Joshua Cogan
ISBN: 9781845230784; pp. 72, April 2009; £7.99

Powerfully illustrated by Joshua Cogan's photographs, Kwame Dawes's poems makes it impossible to see HIV/AIDS as something that only happens to other people. Here, AIDS becomes the channel for dramas that are both universal and unique, voices that are archetypal and highly individual – dramas of despair and stoicism, deception and self-honesty, misery and joy in life.

Anson Gonzalez
Collected Poems
ISBN: 9781845230357; pp. 240, May 2009; £9.99

Those who have followed Anson Gonzalez's career may think they know his evolution from the engaged poet of the politically turbulent Trinidad revealed in *Score*, to the confessional Caribbean Don Juan in *The Love-song of Boysie B.*, to the poet of spiritual exploration in *Moksha: Poems of Light and Sound* and *Merry-go-round and Other Poems*. This new *Collected Poems*, with a number of important new poems, carefully disrupts such expectations by an arrangement that mixes poems from across the decades and reveals an altogether more complex poetic voice.

Millicent A.A. Graham
The Damp in Things
ISBN: 9781845230838; pp. 56, May 2009; £7.99

In *The Damp in Things*, we are invited into the unique imagination of Millicent Graham: she offers us a way to see her distinctly contemporary and urban Jamaica through the slant eye of a surrealist, one willing to see the absurdities and contradictions inherent in its society. These are poems about family, love, spirituality, fear, and above all desire, where the dampness of things is as much about the humid sensuality of this woman's island as it is about her constant belief in fecundity, fertility and the unruliness of the imagination.

Stanley Greaves
The Poems Man
ISBN: 9781845230869; pp. 92, May 2009; £7.99

Written in homage to the great Guyanese poet, Martin Carter, these poems investigate the power of words and the necessity and sanctity of the act of making in the circumstances of disorder that have afflicted Guyana for much of the past half century. Dense and jewelled, these poems create a surreal twist on the everyday and reveal the perceptions of a writer, who is also an artist, sculptor and musician, on the interlinkages between the senses.

Jennifer Rahim
Approaching Sabbaths
ISBN: 9781845231156; pp. 129, July 2009; £8.99

There is a near perfect balance between the disciplined craft of the poems, and their capacity to deal with the most traumatic of experiences in a cool, reflective way. Equally, she has the capacity to make of the ordinary something special and memorable. The threat and reality of fragmentation – of psyches, of lives, of a nation – is ever present, but the shape and order of the poems provide a saving frame of wholeness.

Tanya Shirley
She Who Sleeps with Bones
ISBN: 9781845230876; pp. 76, April 2009; £7.99

'In the deftly searching poems of *She Who Sleeps With Bones*, Tanya Shirley considers how memory revolts from oblivion, what it can mean to be "haunted by the fruit" of desire – sexual, political, the desire for an "uncomplicated legacy," for home when home exists only as a memory we cannot trust entirely, a space we fear even as we continue to go back there. These poems startle, stir, provoke equally with their intelligence and their music. A wonderful debut.'

— Elizabeth Nunez, author of *Prospero's Daughter*

All Peepal Tree titles are available from the website
www.peepaltreepress.com
with a money back guarantee, secure credit card ordering and fast delivery throughout the world at cost or less.

Peepal Tree Press is celebrated as the home of challenging and inspiring literature from the Caribbean and Black Britain. Subscribe to our mailing list for news of new books and events.
Contact us at:
Peepal Tree Press, 17 King's Avenue, Leeds LS6 1QS, UK
Tel: +44 (0) 113 2451703 E-mail: contact@peepaltreepress.com